PUFFIN

PICK OF
From Bug

What sort of animal would you like to keep as a pet? Some are easier to look after than others, and some are a lot bigger than others as well!

Where do you live? Have you got enough space to keep a large Alsatian or would you be better off with a small hamster or mouse? Do you enjoy going for walks or would you prefer to sit back and watch a fish exercising itself in its tank? Would you rather chatter to a budgie as it pecks its seed, or feed scraps to the wild robin on your window ledge?

In this book you can find out all about pets of every shape and size, find out how to look after them, and enjoy games, quizzes, facts and fun all about pets.

Penny Lloyd was born in Chester, went to school in Ellesmere Port and then studied at Manchester University. She has worked in many different areas – community arts, teaching, social work and television – but always with children. She now lives in London with her family.

Penny Lloyd
PICK OF THE PETS
FROM BUGS TO BUNNIES

Illustrated by
Kate Taylor

PUFFIN BOOKS

PUFFIN BOOKS

Published by the Penguin Group
27 Wrights Lane, London W8 5TZ, England
Viking Penguin Inc., 40 West 23rd Street, New York,
New York 10010, USA
Penguin Books Australia Ltd, Ringwood, Victoria, Australia
Penguin Books Canada Ltd, 2801 John Street, Markham,
Ontario, Canada L3R 1B4
Penguin Books (NZ) Ltd, 182–190 Wairau Road, Auckland 10,
New Zealand

Penguin Books Ltd, Registered Offices: Harmondsworth,
Middlesex, England

First published 1990
10 9 8 7 6 5 4 3 2 1

Text copyright © Penny Lloyd, 1990
Illustrations copyright © Kate Taylor, 1990
All rights reserved

The moral right of the author has been asserted

Made and printed in Great Britain by
Cox and Wyman Ltd, Reading, Berks

Filmset in Linotron Meridien by
Rowland Phototypesetting Ltd, Bury St Edmunds, Suffolk

Contents

Odd and Easy Pets

Not enough space at home to keep a pet? Not sure if you want to look after something for a long time? Interested in unusual things? Then try these.

SPIDERS

Have you ever seen a spider either in your house or outside?

Next time you see one, watch it and find out where it lives. Keep a note of what time of day it leaves home. Watch it make its web, and see how long it takes. Don't try to feed it, as spiders are very good at catching their own food, such as flies and insects. If you would like to give it something to drink, try spraying its web very gently with water from a plant spray.

You could give it a name too!

Did You Know?
Every time a spider's web is broken, it has to eat all the silk before it can spin another one.

WOODLICE

Woodlice are very small creatures. Why not try looking after some for a few days?

You will probably find them outdoors under stones, bricks or damp wood, but sometimes you can find them indoors too.

A Woodlouse Home: Woodlice like to live in damp, dark places. Find an old shoebox with a lid, spray the inside of the box with water to keep it damp, and punch a few holes in the lid (they need air too!).

Woodlouse Food: Rotting wood and damp leaves are favourites. Find some and put them in the box for a tasty meal.

• When your woodlouse home and food are ready, gently lift three or four lice with a piece of paper and put them into their new home. So long as you keep the box damp and supplied with food, they will be perfectly happy for four or five days. After this, you will have to say goodbye to your pet woodlice and put them back where you found them.

While you are looking after your woodlice, why not take one on to the palm of your hand for a closer look? Turn it on to its back and watch it turn over again.

Did You Know?
Woodlice are members of the crab family.
Woodlice breathe through their front six legs.

WORMS

Anywhere there is soil there will be worms. If you would like to keep some worms and observe them for a while, you will have to ask someone to help you make a wormery.

How to Make a Wormery

1. Glue three pieces of wood (about 2½ cm thick) together to make a frame.

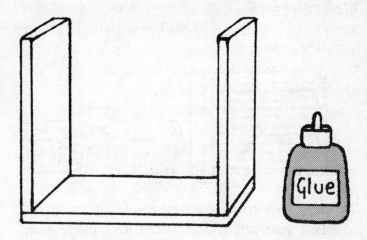

2. Glue a sheet of Perspex to each side of the frame to make a sort of tank.

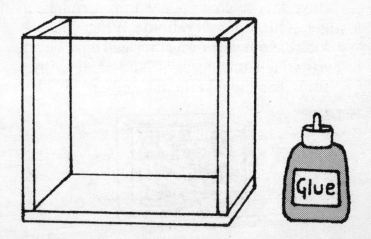

3. When the tank is dry, fill it with alternate layers of damp sand and earth (you can use just earth if you haven't got any sand). Make each layer about 2½ cm thick and leave the same amount of space at the top of the tank.

4. The only thing missing now is the worms!
5. Dig yourself four worms and place them gently on the top layer of earth. Cover the wormery with a dark cloth (worms are at their busiest at night) and leave until the next day, to give your worms a chance to get used to their new home. When you next look at your wormery, they will have begun to plough up the earth and sand as they tunnel and to mix them together.

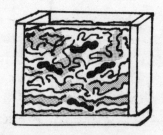

Worm Food: Worms like grass cuttings and dead leaves. Sprinkle some on top of the soil and watch how your worms 'plant' them as they eat them. Sprinkle the surface of the earth regularly with water too.

● Remember worms don't like bright light, so always keep a cloth over the wormery when you are not looking at it.

You can keep your worms indoors for quite a while, but it is kindest to put them back where you found them after a couple of weeks. Always dig a hole and put them deep into the earth, or else they might make a tasty meal for someone!

Did You Know?
Every earthworm has five hearts.
Worms can regrow lost parts of their bodies.

CATERPILLARS

To keep a caterpillar as a pet, you will need patience. If you are lucky, your caterpillar will go to sleep in a pupa and emerge as a butterfly or moth. Two pets in one!

Finding Caterpillars: Become a caterpillar detective and search for evidence of caterpillars among bushes and plants. Look out for nibbled or holey leaves. If you still can't see any caterpillars, then shake the branch gently and catch the caterpillars (and a lot more besides!) on a cloth or large sheet of paper.

A Home for a Caterpillar: A large plastic lunchbox is ideal. If you want to see your caterpillars all the time, then stretch some Clingfilm over the top and pierce some holes in it.

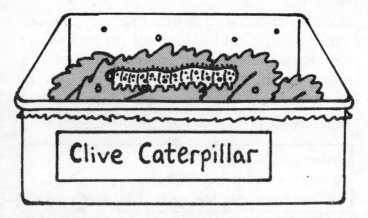

Clive Caterpillar

Caterpillar Food: Your caterpillar will like to eat the leaves of the plant you found it on. Always make sure the food is fresh.

Moulting: If your caterpillar seems tired or off its food, don't worry as it could be going to moult (shed its skin). It may do this more than once and you should never move a caterpillar when it's moulting.

Pupation: If your caterpillar is restless, it may be ready to turn into a butterfly or moth. This is called pupation. Give it some twigs of food, some potting compost and some dry grass so that it can choose where to make its pupa.

● You might have to wait a long time for your butterfly or moth to come out of the pupa. If you are very lucky, you will be able to watch as the wings dry off and harden before it flutters off to lay some more eggs to hatch into caterpillars.

Did You Know?
The silken case that a caterpillar spins around itself when it is turning into a pupa is called a cocoon.
There is a type of caterpillar called a looper because it makes a loop shape when it moves.

SNAILS

You could get to know your snails in the place where they live, or you might like to keep some indoors for a while in an old shoebox with holes in the lid.

First of all, you need to find some snails. Don't look for them in winter because that's when they hibernate. At other times of the year they like to cluster together near large stones, on windowsills or on the sides of buildings. You might find a silvery trail leading to one, or if you're very quiet you might hear one munching a tasty leaf (snails are very noisy eaters!). They eat mostly at night.

How to Tell Who is Who: If you would like to watch a particular snail, or tell which of the ones in your shoebox is which, you could dab a spot of paint on the snail's shell.

Keeping Shoebox Snails: Remember to keep the lid on the box as snails can climb up anything. Give them some food, from the sort of plant that you found them on, sprinkled with water because snails like to be damp.

A Snail Game: You could have a snail race with a friend. Draw a starting and finishing line on the ground with a piece of chalk, but don't draw them too far apart as snails move very slowly! Line your snails up on the starting line. While your snails are racing, watch how they use their eyes (they stick out on stalks on the front of their heads). They can see round corners or even over their own heads.

STICK INSECTS

Have you ever seen a very odd insect that looks like a stick? You might like to keep one as a pet. Stick insects take up very little room and are very cheap to feed. Most pet shops will know where you can buy one, or maybe you know someone with some baby sticks that they want to give away.

Stick Insect Homes: You could use either a tall sweet jar (it must be at least twice as high as the length of the stick insect so that it can moult) covered in muslin cloth, or an old fish tank with a lid with lots of holes in it. Keep it in a warm place (near a radiator is a good spot).

Stick Insect Food: They like bramble, privet or, sometimes, rhododendron leaves. Ask which of these yours likes when you buy it. Stand the stems in a jar of water to keep the leaves moist, and your stick insect will not need a drink.

Stick Insect Care: Clean the jar or tank out every few days and replace the food. Pick up your stick insect carefully by holding the middle part of its body.

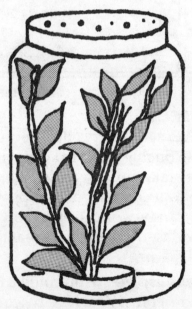

● When your stick insect gets used to its new home, it will move around quite a lot. If it is asleep or resting, it will hang or stand on a twig and might be quite difficult to see.

Babies: Most stick insects are female. They don't need a male to breed with and will lay eggs which will fall to the floor (they look like hard droppings). If you save some eggs when you clean out and keep them on some damp sand in a small jar of their own, they will eventually hatch into babies which can join your other sticks.

Some Sticky Facts: Stick insects have sticky bits on the ends of their feet for holding on to things. Perhaps that's another reason why they're called stick insects!

• They use their antennae to smell their food so they can tell what they're eating.

Can you think of an interesting name for a stick insect? (In America they're called walking sticks.)

THE BIRDS ON YOUR WINDOWSILL

Wherever you live you will have a window. Have a look and see if there are any birds (it doesn't matter if you don't know what they are). If you would like to have a closer look at them, then offer them some food.

Ideas For Bird Food

Bread.

Scraps from your meals.

Half a coconut hung up on a piece of string.

Wild birds can be very timid, so don't be disappointed if they don't come to the food straight away. Keep trying, it may take as long as a week. When they do come to eat, keep very still and quiet or you will frighten them away. Soon they will know that they are safe and will visit your window often.

If you decide you enjoy watching the birds, then you could make a scrap bag.

A Scrap Bag: You will need a piece of string, a plastic mesh bag (oranges are sometimes sold in them) and some food scraps.

● Fill the bag with scraps, tie string around the top and hang it from your window. The birds will come and peck through the holes.

Remember, you should only feed birds in winter, as in summer they can find plenty of food for themselves. They will quickly rely on you, so you must feed them regularly. It is also a good idea to give them a bowl of fresh

water daily. Stop feeding gradually when the weather gets warmer.

In the spring you could leave out some nesting materials instead of food, to help the birds make their nests.

Nesting Materials

Wool.
Paper scraps.
String.
Straw.
Old leaves and twigs.
Feathers.

Try filling your scrap bag with these instead of food and still see your 'pets' at your window in springtime.

Birdy Questions

Who am I?

1. Small and brown with a white tummy and a red breast.
2. Black with a yellow beak.
3. Small with a yellow tummy, blue hat, black collar and blue wings.
4. You will know it is spring when you hear me sing.

Answers
1. Robin. 2. Male blackbird.
3. Bluetit. 4. Cuckoo.

Odd and Easy Crossword

CLUES

Across
1. A place to observe worms.
2. Snails might like to eat by the light of the _____.
3. A spring bird.

Down
1. A spider's meal.
2. A caterpillar spins this.
3. Useful to make nests with.

Wet Pets

Fish are quite cheap to keep and beautiful to look at. They do need to be looked after carefully though, so before buying your fish you will need to buy some equipment. This will be the most expensive part of fish keeping and you will need to ask an adult to help you set it up.

COLD-WATER OR TROPICAL FISH?

Which sort would you like to keep? Cold-water fish are probably easier because they need less equipment, but there are more types of tropical fish that you can keep in a tank, so your display will look more colourful.

Here are some fish that you can keep

COLD-WATER

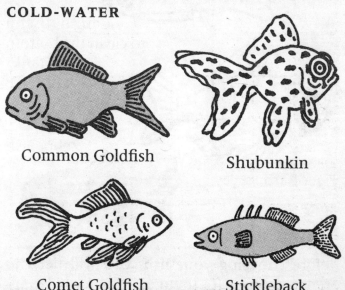

Common Goldfish

Shubunkin

Comet Goldfish

Stickleback

TROPICAL

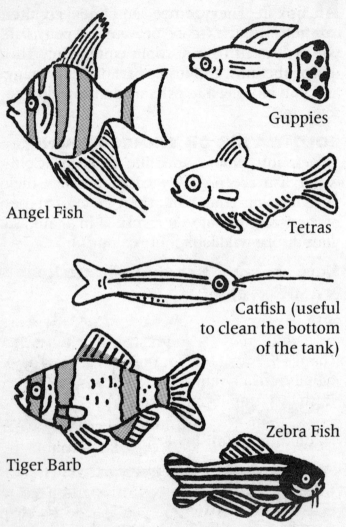

Guppies

Angel Fish

Tetras

Catfish (useful to clean the bottom of the tank)

Zebra Fish

Tiger Barb

Before choosing your fish, you will need to prepare a home for them.

FISH HOMES

All fish need oxygen to live. They get their oxygen from the water they live in. You should never keep fish in a bowl, because it only has a little opening and the water does not get enough oxygen. You will need to buy a tank.

TANKS

How big a tank will you need? That depends on how many fish you have, but it is always better to buy one that is too big rather than too small. A tank 60 cm wide, 38 cm long and 30 cm deep will be big enough for about fifteen tropical fish or four goldfish.

TANK FURNITURE

Air Pump: The fresher the water, the more oxygen there is for your fish. You could either change the water in your tank every few days, or buy an air pump which keeps the water fresh by pumping air through it.

Filter: This is useful to help keep the water clean, especially if you keep a lot of fish.

Water Heater and Thermostat: Tropical fish come from warm countries and need to live in warm water. If you decide to keep tropical fish, you will need to buy a water heater to heat the water and a thermostat to control the temperature of the water.

Lid: A lid for your tank will help stop dust falling into the water (and help stop any other pets from taking the fish!). You can buy a lid with holes in or you can make one from a sheet of glass. Put a ball of Plasticine on each corner of the tank and place a sheet of glass the same size as the tank on top. The Plasticine will lift the glass so that air can get in.

WHERE TO PUT YOUR TANK

A tank full of water is too heavy to lift, so decide where you want to put your tank before you fill it. Remember that whatever you stand the tank on must be strong enough to hold it when it is full.

Put your tank in a fairly light place (you can put an artificial light in the lid), but don't put it near a window because the sun shining through the glass will make the water too hot. Don't place it next to a radiator or fire either!

DECORATING YOUR TANK

Why not design a sort of water garden in which your fish can swim and play around?

Gravel: You can buy fish-tank gravel in many different colours, so you can design your own colour scheme. Wash it thoroughly in cold water first to remove any dirt or grit. Then put a layer about 5 cm deep along the bottom of your tank. This will give you something to plant things in as well.

Plants: There are many different aquarium plants available, so it is up to you to choose those which suit your design best. As well as looking colourful, plants put oxygen in the water and give the fish somewhere to hide. Remember that the more you plant, the less easy it will be for you to see your fish!

● Bury the roots of plants among the gravel. You could also add pebbles or shells as decoration.

FILLING THE TANK

Cover your plants and gravel with a layer of paper to keep them in place and gently fill the tank with tap-water.

Leave the tank for about a week so that the water can age before putting your fish in. This is very important.

CHOOSING YOUR FISH

Always check that a fish is healthy before buying it and try to buy only from someone with a good reputation. Healthy fish should:

1. Have perfect fins.
2. Swim easily.
3. Have clear eyes lying flat, not sunken or sticking out.
4. Have an undamaged body.
5. Have a bright colour.

Look out for tiny white spots or fluffy patches. If a fish has these, do not buy it.

Fish naturally swim in groups, so your fish will be happiest if it has company. If you are buying more than one type of fish, check with the shopkeeper that the types will get on together – some fish are bullies!

PUTTING YOUR FISH INTO THEIR NEW HOME

You will probably take your fish home in a plastic bag filled with water, tied tightly so that air is trapped at the top. At home, float the bag in the water in your tank for about ten minutes, then open it gently. Use your thermometer to check that the water inside and outside the bag is the same temperature, then slowly tip the bag and let your fish swim into their new home. Watch them explore.

They might be upset by their journey, so it

is best not to feed them until the following morning.

FOOD
You can buy special fish food from a pet shop. Sprinkle a pinch of food on the surface of the water. Feeding rules are:

1. Never overfeed as this can kill the fish.
2. Only give the fish more if they still seem hungry.
3. Give your fish an occasional special treat. They usually love live daphnia (water fleas) which you can buy from a pet shop.
4. Always clear away any uneaten food.

CLEANING YOUR TANK
Each week remove and replace about one-fifth of the water. Before putting fresh tap-water into your tank, always leave it standing for a day. Check the temperature of the water, because sudden temperature changes will shock your fish and may kill them.

If the side of your tank looks green, this is because algae are growing there. Algae are very small green plants, which you may notice the fish nibbling at from time to time. You can buy a special scraper to clean algae off the glass, or, if you would like to employ a cleaner, put some water snails in your tank. They like eating algae and will keep the glass clean!

HANDLING FISH

Never ever touch fish with dry hands, because this will damage them. If you do need to move your fish, always use two nets – one to guide the fish and the other to catch them. Never tip a fish out of the net; always lower the net into the water and let the fish swim out of it.

HEALTH

If you keep your tank clean and the water fresh, your fish should be healthy. If you do notice any fish looking unwell or showing signs of disease, then ask your vet's advice straight away. You will find out where your nearest vet is if you look in the *Yellow Pages* telephone directory.

● Fish are very sensitive to vibrations, so don't play loud music too near them or tap the glass. Watch them instead. How do they swim? How do they eat? How do they sleep? Can you see them 'talking' to each other, or playing together?

Did You Know?
When fish swim together in a group it is called a school.
Baby fish are called fry.

A Fishy Quiz

1. As well as food, what do fish need to stay alive?
2. What is a filter for?
3. What are algae?
4. Which tropical fish helps to clean the tank?
5. Which other tank creature is also a cleaner?
6. How can you tell a healthy fish?
7. What are daphnia?
8. How many different types of fish can you name?

(Answers to these questions are all in this chapter.)

Feathered Friends

If you enjoy watching the birds on your windowsill, why not get to know a bird better by keeping a budgerigar or a canary as a pet? They are colourful to look at and good company, especially budgies who can be very noisy! Male canaries sing beautifully and a budgie might even be persuaded to say a few words.

BUYING YOUR BIRD

It is always safest to buy a bird from a well-known dealer. If you would like to try taming a budgie or canary then only buy one, otherwise the bird will be more interested in its playmate than in listening to you. If you do decide to buy more than one, two males (cocks) will get on best.

Cock budgies learn to talk more easily than hens (females). You can tell them apart as the cock has a blue piece of flesh above its beak called a cere. A hen's cere is brown. A cock canary sings best too, but it is very difficult to tell cock canaries from hens. The dealer will help you.

Make sure that the bird you buy:

1. Is sleek and well groomed.
2. Has full and healthy plumage (feathers).
3. Is bright-eyed, alert and inquisitive.
4. Is interested in its food.
5. Is playful with its cage mates.

6. Has firm droppings – black and white, never yellow or green.

If a bird looks puffed up and tired, it may be just sleepy. Watch it when it is asleep. How many legs does it sleep on? If it sleeps on one leg, it is probably healthy. An ill bird will sleep on two legs!

BIRD HOUSING

Choose a cage with lots of room. All-metal ones are most common, but they can be very draughty. So if you choose an all-metal cage, be careful to place it away from draughts and out of direct sunlight.

Wooden-box cages with metal bars at the front are less draughty. The door of a cage should always be big enough to move the bird in and out on your finger without touching the sides.

Covering the Cage: Budgies, in particular, are very active for about twelve hours during the day, then they need a rest. To calm them down, cover the cage with a cloth to make them think it's night-time.

CAGE FURNITURE

Perches: Budgies and canaries like climbing, so why not build your bird a home gym? Fix some perches and a small ladder in the cage. You can buy ready-made wooden perches, but twigs of different sizes are just as good (make sure the wood is dry). Your bird will exercise its feet by hopping up and down the ladder and holding on to the perches, and its beak by gnawing the bark.

Food Containers: Some cages have food containers attached to the bars. Otherwise, use two small plastic dishes. Place them away from the perches or droppings will fall into them.

Water Container: A bowl similar to the food bowl can be filled with fresh water every day, or you could buy a plastic water dispenser which will fit on to the bars of the cage and keep the water clean.

Carpet: Carpet the floor of your cage with newspaper or brown paper to catch the droppings. Sprinkle the paper with a bit of sand. You can buy special sandpaper which is more absorbent, but it may make your bird's feet sore.

Toys: Very important! Try a small mirror (budgies particularly like these), ping-pong balls, or a bell to play a tune with. Don't put too many toys in the cage or your bird will keep bumping into things! Always remove anything if it is broken or your bird might hurt itself.

FOOD

Budgies and canaries like to eat little and often so make sure some seed, at least, is always available. You can buy budgie seed and canary seed from a pet shop (canary seed is oilier). As the birds eat the seed they leave the husks behind, so try to remember to blow the husks off the top of the dish every day or they will hide the seed.

They also like to eat fruit and greens. Experiment to see which is your bird's favourite. Try dandelion, cabbage or lettuce leaves, and pieces of orange or apple. Canaries particularly like scraped carrot or tomato. Always wash any fresh food carefully and remove any unwanted food from the cage before it goes stale.

Water: Always make sure clean fresh water is available, although you won't see your bird drinking very often. As an experiment, put a few drops of water on a cabbage leaf and watch what happens!

Cuttlefish Bone: You can buy cuttlefish bone from a pet shop and wedge it between the bars of the cage. It will help your bird to wear down its beak as well as give it calcium.

CLEANING OUT

Change the paper on the floor of the cage whenever it looks dirty (twice a week is probably enough). Some cages have a tray at the bottom that slides out to make cleaning easier.

Wash and dry the bottom of the cage once a week, and it is also a good idea to wash the cage bars occasionally and replace the dirty perches. Ask an adult to destroy the old ones for you.

HEALTH

If your bird's beak or claws grow too long and need clipping, or if it seems at all ill, ask your vet for help. Watch out for watery eyes, runny nose, diarrhoea or fleas.

MOULTING

Don't worry if your bird loses its feathers. This is quite normal and is called moulting.

Canaries moult for about a month at the end of each summer. When they are moulting, they like to have a bath. Offer them a shallow dish of water in the mornings and watch how they wash themselves. They will have plenty of time to dry out by evening and won't catch cold.

Budgies don't moult as regularly as canaries, but will moult around October if at all.

TAMING YOUR BIRD

If you would like to tame your bird, buy a canary with smooth legs or a budgie with barred markings on its forehead, as these are signs of youth. Canaries are not as friendly as budgies and don't really like being handled, so they aren't as easy to tame.

As soon as your bird has settled into its new home, begin to talk gently to it. It may take a few 'chats' before it takes any notice of you, but when it does you can begin to handle it. Always be gentle and don't make any sudden movements or you will frighten it. Put your hand slowly into the cage, stroke the bird's chest and offer it your finger. Don't try to force it.

When your bird is used to sitting on your finger, try bringing it out of the cage.

First of all:

1. Shut all doors and windows.
2. Close the curtains so it won't try to escape and fly into the glass.
3. Take other pets out of the room.
4. Put a guard over the fire.

Soon you will be able to stroke your bird and offer it daily exercise sessions. Birds are healthier and may live longer if they are allowed to fly freely. It is a good idea to exercise your bird when it is hungry, as you can then use food to tempt it back into its cage.

HOLDING A BIRD
If you need to hold your bird for any reason, close your palm very gently round its back and hold its head between your thumb and first finger. Never squeeze it.

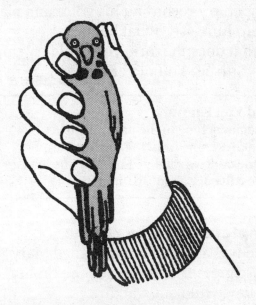

TALKING TO YOUR BUDGIE
Not all budgies talk and cocks talk more easily than hens. There's no harm in trying anyway!

Budgies copy all sorts of sounds – doorbells, telephones, whistling. They can take you by surprise, so be careful what you say! Try your budgie with simple words first, and repeat them until it copies you. After a while you might find you have an echo! Try to chat to your budgie every day.

SINGALONG WITH YOUR CANARY

Cocks sing best. Your canary actually sings because he is rivalling another cock. If your canary does not have a rival because he is your only pet, try recording his voice and playing it back to him – see what happens!

If that doesn't work, you could try singing to him yourself. You never know . . .

Did You Know?
Budgies belong to the parrot family.
Canaries come from the Canary Isles.
Some budgies can live for up to fifteen years (most live for about six though).

Complete this silly rhyme

There was a young budgie called Mary
Whose great friend was Joe the canary
One day while out walking
Mary got talking
And _____.

Small Pets

Would you like to look after a small creature that you can tame, that doesn't take up too much space, doesn't cost a lot to feed and is easy to care for? That can exercise itself without wearing you out? Then why not try a rabbit, a guinea pig, a mouse, a hamster or a gerbil? They are all very entertaining, but the only drawback is that none of them lives for very long. Rabbits live the longest at about six to eight years, guinea pigs and hamsters about three years, gerbils between three and five years, and mice only two years.

Mouse

Rabbit

Gerbil

Guinea Pig

Hamster

RABBITS

Rabbits can live outdoors or indoors, although they are usually kept outdoors. They never make a noise and don't smell, but they do like you to give them lots of attention, exercise and conversation (as well as food, of course!). They are easy to tame and handle and live for six to eight years.

BUYING A RABBIT

It is always best to buy a rabbit from a dealer with a good reputation. The younger the rabbit, the easier it will be to tame, so choose a nine- to twelve-week-old with bright eyes and smooth, clean fur.

There are many different types of rabbit to choose from. Here are some of them:

Dutch

Himalayan

Angora

Chinchilla

French Lop

English

The larger breeds of rabbit can be very heavy so, unless you are very strong, you will probably find a smaller one easier to handle. Rabbits do like company, but always choose two of the same sex and from the same litter or else they will either have lots of babies or fight fiercely!

RABBIT HOMES

Rabbit houses are called hutches. It is expensive to give your rabbit a nice hutch, but it is the most costly part of rabbit keeping. A rabbit needs a strong wooden hutch, fairly big because rabbits like to hop around a lot. For a medium-sized rabbit, the hutch should be at least 100 cm long, 60 cm wide and 60 cm high. The rabbit needs a bedroom and a living room. The bedroom should have a solid wooden door to keep it warm, and the living room a wire mesh door to let the light in. The hutch should be raised off the ground to keep it dry and to keep other animals away, and the roof should be covered in waterproof material and slope backwards so that rain can drain away.

POSITION OF HUTCH

Put your hutch out of direct sunlight so that the rabbit doesn't get too warm in summer, and in a sheltered position away from draughts. Put a loose cover over the living-room end at night if the weather is very cold, or best of all take the hutch indoors into a shed or garage.

FURNITURE

Bed: Give your rabbit a thin layer of bedding in the living room, and a much thicker layer in the bedroom. You can make the bedding from

sawdust, wood shavings, straw, hay or shredded paper.

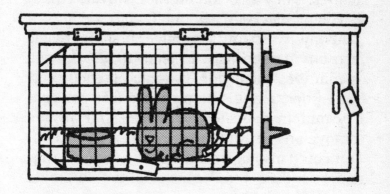

Food Bowls: Give your rabbit a heavy pot-
tery food bowl that can't be knocked over. You
can use the same sort of bowl for water but a
proper water bottle, hung upside down from
the mesh door, would be best as it would keep
the water clean.

FOOD
Rabbits like two meals a day, one in the
morning and one in the evening.

Breakfast: Make a rabbit muesli of rabbit
pellets, crushed oats, barley, maize flakes and
wheat, all of which you can buy from a pet
shop. Or, for a special treat, make a rabbit mash
by mixing hot milk with cereal, wholemeal
bread or cooked potato peelings.

43

Supper: Rabbits like to eat lots of vegetables. Try cabbage, beetroot, carrots, celery or dandelions. They also like nettles, clover, chickweed and blackberry bramble.

Always wash any vegetables first and never feed any garden or wild plant to your rabbit as many of them, for example bluebells and buttercups, are poisonous. Make sure you give hay and fresh water every day and always remove any uneaten food before it goes stale. You could also buy your rabbit a mineral ring to lick, and tie it to the inside of the hutch – a sort of rabbit lollipop!

CLEANING OUT

Clean droppings away every day. A scraper is useful for this. If your rabbit has a favourite toilet place, you could put a shallow baking tray under the bedding. It would then be easier to take the droppings away. Change the bedding completely every week and scrub the hutch out from time to time with mild disinfectant. Always make sure that it is completely dry before putting the rabbit back in.

EXERCISE

Your rabbit needs daily exercise. Some people like to let their rabbits roam about their house rather like a cat or dog. Whether you decide to do this or not is up to you, although it is probably wise to have an adult's permission first. If you do let your rabbit roam about, you will have some cleaning up to do afterwards!

If your rabbit is very tame and you have a garden, then you might be able to let him loose outside. Rabbits do like burrowing though and have been known to dig their way under fences and escape! The safest way to exercise your rabbit would be to make, or buy, a run for him. The best sort of run is called a Morant Hutch and looks like this.

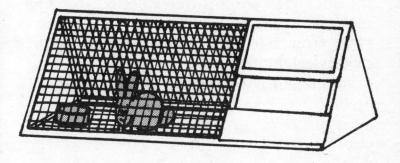

The mesh on the floor allows the rabbit to eat grass, but prevents him burrowing into the lawn and escaping.

PLAYTHINGS

Experiment! Try giving your rabbit a tray of earth to dig in so that he can, at least, indulge his burrowing urges, even if they don't get him very far! A piece of old drainpipe or chimney-pot might also be fun.

RABBIT HABITS

At night rabbits pass different droppings to those passed in the daytime. These are dark green, soft and shiny. Don't worry if you see your rabbit eating these droppings, as it is quite normal and is a very important part of his digestion called refecation.

HANDLING

Never lift a rabbit by the ears, always use two hands – one under his bottom and one to hold the ears and loose skin behind the neck. If your rabbit is very tame, you might be able to put your second hand under his chest. Make your rabbit feel more secure by letting him lie against your chest while you are holding him.

Protect yourself! Rabbits have very strong hind legs and may kick or scratch you, so always lift your rabbit out of the hutch with his head towards you.

As well as feeding and exercising your rabbit, it is very important to give him a cuddle and have a chat with him every day so that he doesn't get lonely.

DOES OR BUCKS?

Male rabbits are called bucks and female rabbits are called does. If you would like to know which sex your rabbit is, cradle it in your arms like a baby and, with the help of an adult, press very gently on each side of the opening furthest away from the tail. A buck has got a round opening and a doe a slit-shaped opening.

47

Never keep a buck and a doe together or you will have an endless supply of babies! In fact, it is probably best not to try breeding rabbits at all unless you have a lot of space and a number of spare cages to put the babies into.

Babies: If you think your doe might be expecting babies, look after her well and give her plenty to eat and drink.

• Usually between five and ten babies will be born. This is called a litter. The babies will leave the nest when they are about twenty days old. Until then, don't handle them or the mother may reject them.

As well as drinking milk from their mother, they will also eat her food and drink her water, so give her extra. Separate the babies from the mother at about seven weeks old and put the doe and buck babies in separate cages.

Now all you need to do is look after the babies well until you can find them good homes.

HEALTH

Rabbits are usually quite healthy but look out for discharge from the ears; overgrown nails or teeth; snuffles or runny eyes. If in doubt, ask your vet for help.

Did You Know?
In the wild, rabbits come out of their burrows at dawn and dusk to feed.
Angora rabbit fur can be clipped and spun into soft wool for jumpers.
Rabbits get on well with guinea pigs. They can even share the same hutch.

GUINEA PIGS

Guinea pigs are extremely noisy, chatty and companionable animals. They are smaller than rabbits, easy to handle and to tame. Guinea pigs can be kept outdoors in a sheltered spot, but are more often housed indoors in a shed or garage.

CHOOSING A GUINEA PIG

Always buy from a good dealer. A healthy guinea pig should:
1. Have a firm, well-rounded body.
2. Have soft smooth fur.
3. Have bright eyes.
4. Breathe quietly.
5. Have clean ears, nose and mouth.

It is best to buy a guinea pig aged between four and six weeks old. Guinea pigs really do enjoy company. If you can buy two guinea pigs, choose two females (sows) as two males (boars) will fight.

There are three main breeds to choose from:

1. English (short and smooth haired).

2. Abyssinian (rough tufted hair).

3. Peruvian (long silky hair).

GUINEA PIG HOUSING

Two guinea pigs can live happily in an ordinary rabbit hutch with separate living and sleeping rooms. A guinea-pig hutch should not be left outside in cold weather, as guinea pigs can catch cold easily. So, if you normally would keep the hutch in a garden or yard, then it is a good idea to ask someone to help you bring it indoors when the weather gets cold.

FURNITURE

Bedding: Hay makes comfortable guinea-pig bedding, so loosely fill the sleeping compartment with it.

Living Room: Carpet the living-room floor with newspaper and cover this with a good layer of clean sawdust.

Food Bowls: Put a small bowl for food in the living room. Guinea pigs aren't as strong as rabbits, so the bowls needn't be as heavy. A water bottle (as for rabbits) is the cleanest way of giving water.

FOOD

Guinea pigs are nibblers and like to eat throughout the day, so you should always leave some food for them. Their diet is practically the same as a rabbit's, which is convenient if you keep both together. They do need extra vitamin C, so feed them pieces of orange as well. For variety you can buy special guinea-pig food from a pet shop. Always be sure to remove any stale food from the hutch.

EXERCISE

You can exercise your guinea pig in a rabbit run. Guinea pigs don't burrow like rabbits do, so it isn't necessary to have mesh on the bottom. Guinea pigs need daily exercise, but always make sure that they are not in danger from dogs or cats.

HANDLING

Guinea pigs are quite nervous and timid at first, so gradually handle yours until she gets used to you. Pick her up by sliding your hand under her body and place your other hand on top to steady her. Guinea pigs are famous for falling off things, so take care. They can hurt themselves badly even if they don't fall far.

TALKING

Listen to all the different sounds your guinea pig makes. You will soon learn which sounds are happy and which complaining.

SOWS OR BOARS?

You can tell the sex of your guinea pig in the same way as that of a rabbit.

Don't keep a sow and a boar together or you will have lots of guinea piglets. If your sow is expecting babies, you should look after her well. She will have three or four babies in her litter. Look after the litter as you would a rabbit's.

HEALTH

Guinea pigs are healthy animals and usually live for about three years. Look out for signs of a cold; diarrhoea; loss of appetite; difficulty breathing or moving; over-long teeth or nails. If you think your guinea pig is ill, ask a vet for help.

Did You Know?
Guinea pigs are really called 'cavies', and come from South America.
When a sow guinea pig is expecting babies, it is called being 'in pig'.

MICE

There are many different colours of pet mouse from which to choose. The most common are Pink Eyed Whites, which, as you might expect, are white mice with pink eyes. The disadvantage of keeping mice is that they can be smelly. You will need to clean them out thoroughly at least twice a week.

CHOOSING A MOUSE

Healthy mice have sleek shiny coats and firm bodies. They are alert and inquisitive. You can buy mice from pet shops, but it is probably best to buy one from a breeder. Mice like company. If you keep one mouse on its own, it will be very lonely and will probably not live as long as it would if it had a companion. Two females will get on best of all. Two males will fight, and it is best not to keep a male and a female together or you will have lots of babies to find homes for.

A MOUSE HOUSE

Mice are busy and lively creatures, so you will need to provide them with a house that is big enough to run around in. A cage for two mice should be at least 60 cm long, 30 cm wide and 30 cm high.

You can buy metal or wooden cages. Metal ones are gnawproof, wooden ones are warmest. You could use an aquarium with a mesh lid, but this might get rather smelly as there would be no ventilation. Put the cage indoors away from draughts, and make sure that no cat can reach it or you might have a dead mouse on your hands (or at least a very frightened one!).

FURNITURE

Mice like their furniture to be on lots of different levels, so try to buy a cage with several different floors, or ask an adult to help you make some. Remember mice have sharp teeth and can easily gnaw through thin wood.

Carpet: Spread a layer of wood shavings or sawdust over the floor of the cage.

Bed: On the top floor put a nesting box for your mice to sleep in. Give them some hay or straw, rags or paper as bedding.

Stairs: If your mouse house has several floors, give your mice some ladders (you can buy them in pet shops) or ramps to get from one floor to another.

Food Bowls: You will need to provide some small earthenware bowls and an upside-down water bottle.

Toys: Mice are busy creatures and need toys to keep them occupied. They might like a wheel to exercise in. Make sure that it is a solid one with no spokes, so no tails can get stuck. Try giving them some ropes to climb up or old cardboard tubes to run in and out of. For gnawing toys you could provide an old plastic cotton reel (too hard to gnaw through), a piece of wood with some bark or some acorns.

FOOD

Mice like to eat twice a day, morning and early evening. They do love cheese, but it is best not to feed it to them as it makes them very smelly! Mouse pellets can be bought from a pet shop. In fact, they will eat almost anything but you should encourage them to eat a balanced diet.

Breakfast: Mice like oats, about one teaspoonful per day per mouse. They can be mixed with bran, canary seed (don't expect them to sing though!) or cornflakes.

Supper: In the evening mice like vegetables – lettuce, cabbage, dandelion leaves, raw carrot or turnip, and a mash of wholemeal bread and milk.

● Always remove any uneaten food from the cage and don't overfeed – fat mice aren't healthy mice.

CLEANING OUT

Clean out the cage twice a week using a scraper and a scrubbing brush. Rinse everything well in hot water. You will need an escape-proof box to put your mice in while cleaning out. Try a shoebox with a tight-fitting lid and holes in. Wash food bowls every day.

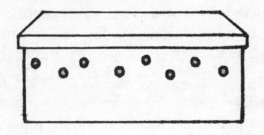

HANDLING

To pick your mouse up, take hold of her tail gently by the widest part near the body and lift her bottom up. Slide your other hand under the mouse and pick her up. Never make sudden movements or hold her round the body, as you will frighten her and she may bite.

EXERCISE

Because mice are always busy and on the go, they give themselves plenty of exercise. They do enjoy being handled and stroked though, so you should play with them every day. A very tame mouse will even enjoy exploring your pockets.

DOES OR BUCKS?

It is not easy with mice to tell a buck from a doe. This is how you could try. Hold the mouse on your hand and lift the tail end by the wide bit. In the buck the two openings under the tail are further apart than they are in the doe.

BABIES

Mice breed very quickly and a litter may have as many as eighteen babies. Unless you want to fill your house with cages, it is probably best to leave breeding to others.

If your doe does have babies, don't touch the litter or the mother may reject the babies and eat them. At four weeks old the babies will eat the same kind of food as their mother so the same feeding rules apply, although once a day is probably enough. At seven weeks separate the bucks from the does and put them in different cages.

HEALTH

If you take care of your mouse and her diet, she should be healthy. Mice are quite fragile creatures though, so look out for wheezing, swellings, bare patches, sores or colds. If you think a mouse is ill, take it to your vet.

Did You Know?
Baby mice are born without hair and with their eyes and ears closed. Their eyes open when they are twelve days old.

HAMSTERS

Hamsters are busy, soft, scurrying, playful little animals with short tails and very friendly faces. They are very quiet unless frightened, when they make a sort of high-pitched squeak. The drawback to hamster keeping is that hamsters are nocturnal. Although you will see them in the daytime, they are at their most lively and sociable at night.

CHOOSING A HAMSTER

There are several species of hamster, but the one most often kept as a pet is the golden hamster. In spite of its name, there are many different colours of golden hamster from which to choose. Whichever colour you buy, make sure the hamster is well rounded and sturdy with bright eyes and soft fur, and that the fur underneath its tail is dry. Choose a young one as hamsters don't live long! Young hamsters have very small white hairs inside their ears.

● Most small pets like company. Hamsters definitely don't. Two hamsters of any sex will fight fiercely, so only buy one. Males are slightly less aggressive than females.

A HAMSTER HOUSE

Hamsters have very strong teeth for gnawing, so metal or glass cages are most practical as they are gnawproof. The cage should be at least 60 cm long, 30 cm wide and 30 cm high. Some hamster houses are rather like palaces, being circular and on several floors.

Hamsters come from a warm country, so keep the cage indoors in a warm place.

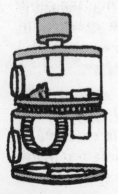 

FURNITURE

Carpet: Cover the floor with a layer of sawdust.

Bed: Hamsters like to build nests so you will need to make a bed area, which could be a nesting box. Give your hamster plenty of bedding to build with – woodchips, shredded paper or hay but not cotton wool.

Toilet: Your hamster will probably go to the toilet in the same place every day. To make cleaning easier, you could put a tin lid under the sawdust in that position or an old jam-jar on its side.

Food Bowls: You will need to provide a small heavy bowl and an upside-down water bottle.

Toys: As hamsters live alone, they very much enjoy playing. So you can give your hamster lots of toys. Try old cotton reels or pine cones to chew, cardboard tubes to climb through, or a short piece of rope. An exercise wheel is a good idea, so long as it is a safe one with no holes for a tail or a foot to get stuck in.

FOOD

You can buy hamster food from pet shops. This is actually very good. Hamsters also like greens, lettuce, dandelion leaves, and pieces of apple. Never give them citrus fruits (oranges, grapefruit or lemons).

As a treat, you could occasionally give your hamster small pieces of hard-boiled egg, or lean, cooked meat.

Always make sure there is fresh water.

HAMSTER HABITS

If your hamster seems to eat a lot of food very quickly and then looks as if he has got a bad case of the mumps, don't worry! Hamsters have a pouch in each cheek which they can stuff full of food and then empty in some secret hiding-place to eat later on. When you clean the cage, you will probably find this secret larder!

CLEANING OUT

Clean the cage thoroughly once a week, but remove any damp sawdust every day. In the summer you could put your hamster in a run (like a guinea-pig run, only with smaller mesh) while you do this, or give him to someone to hold.

HANDLING

Offer your hamster food from your hand, so that he gets used to you before you try to pick him up. Remember that hamsters are very short-sighted, so always approach them slowly and quietly or they will be frightened and bite. If you point a finger at them to tickle their nose, they will think it is food and bite it – so be careful!

Pick your hamster up by wrapping your hand gently around his body. Don't let him fall or the injury could be serious. You may get bitten a few times, but your hamster will soon get used to you and become very tame. Once your hamster is really tame, he will sit on your hand to wash himself.

EXERCISE

A hamster, like a mouse, will get plenty of exercise scurrying around his cage, but he might also like a bit of freedom. Once he is really tame, you might like to let him go for a walk on the carpet, sit on your knee or ride in your pocket.

If, by some mischance, you lose your hamster among the furniture, you can catch him in a tall jam-jar. Leave it propped up so that it slopes, put some hay and sawdust inside and some food. When your hamster is hungry he will climb into the jar for food, but he won't be able to climb out again. You can use this 'trap' on mice and gerbils too.

MALE OR FEMALE?

Look at the shape of your hamster's tail. The male's body is rounded from the back legs in a big bulge down to the tail, whereas the female's body is pointed.

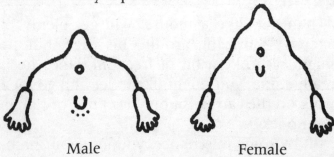

Male   Female

BABIES

Because a hamster has a fighting nature and has to live alone, it is unlikely that you will find your female hamster unexpectedly having babies. It is better to leave breeding to the experts!

HEALTH

Hamsters are usually very healthy. If in cold weather your hamster looks as if he is dead, he may have gone into hibernation. You should warm your hamster in your hand and take him to a warm place. After about forty-five minutes, he should wake up slowly. When he seems fully awake, offer him a drink of warm sweet milk. Never wake him up suddenly or the shock will be too great.

Other illnesses to keep an eye out for are overgrown or broken teeth; wounds from fighting; irritated skin; colds; or diarrhoea. See your vet if you think your hamster is ill.

Did You Know?
When hamsters are sleepy their ears lie flat.
All pet golden hamsters are descended from three found in the Syrian deserts in 1930.

GERBILS

Gerbils are inquisitive, entertaining and very lively. They are cheap to keep (they don't eat much!), very healthy and they don't smell. Their only disadvantage is that because they are so lively, they can easily escape while you are handling them.

CHOOSING A GERBIL

Mongolian gerbils are the most popular to keep as pets, with golden brown fur and long tails. Choose a gerbil with a shiny coat and bright eyes. It is essential to buy two gerbils together as they hate to be lonely. Their territory is then always shared, and they don't fight. Any combination of male and female will get on well, but if you keep a male and female pair you will be overrun by babies. A female gerbil will have about fifteen litters a year! It is probably best to keep two females, as males sometimes fight.

GERBIL HOMES

Gerbils can live in solid wooden cages with a glass front and wire netting on top. As gerbils like to burrow in the wild and burrowing can

be interesting to watch, a glass aquarium 60 cm long, 30 cm wide and 30 cm high and covered with a lid of wire mesh makes an interesting gerbilarium. Gerbils like to stand on their hind legs and stretch, so make sure the height of the gerbilarium allows this. The gerbilarium can be kept anywhere indoors, but avoid placing it in direct sunlight. Gerbils adapt to changes in temperature quite well.

FURNITURE

Carpet: Cover the floor with a large amount of litter. Litter can be made from sand, sawdust, peat, hay and woodshavings. Bank it up towards the back of the tank to give depth for burrowing.

Bed: The gerbils will make their own bedroom by burrowing. Give them some hay or clean kitchen paper to shred and make a bed with.

Food Containers: Provide an upside-down water bottle strung from the mesh lid, and a heavy food bowl that can't be tipped up.

Toys: Gerbils like to be busy. They love shredding clean paper and cardboard tubes (this makes a tremendous noise!). They also like shredding clean cotton rags. Jam-jars make good tunnels, and they enjoy gnawing twigs. Do not give gerbils exercise wheels because their long tails can get trapped.

FOOD

Gerbils eat much the same sort of food as hamsters. They love sunflower seeds, but don't give them too many. They also need a daily portion of vegetables, which may include lettuce, turnip, spinach and cauliflower. Particular favourites are apples and watermelon seeds. Gerbils need fresh water every day, even though they might not drink much of it.

CLEANING OUT

Always make sure the glass inside the gerbilarium is dry and clean. Gerbil droppings are dry and do not smell, so the gerbilarium only needs cleaning out completely every three to four weeks. Wash and thoroughly dry it before renewing litter and bedding. Each time you do this, you will be able to watch your gerbils digging new burrows.

Cake Tin.

While cleaning your gerbilarium, put your gerbils somewhere safe so that they can't escape – a dry bath with the plug in or a large cake tin. A shoebox is no use because they will shred it.

HANDLING

To pick up your gerbil, put some food in the palm of your hand and offer it to her. She will then climb on to the palm of your hand to get the food. Then grasp the base of her tail, as near to the body as possible, with the thumb and first finger and hold the gerbil on the palm of your hand. Lifting by any other part of the tail

will damage her. Gerbils are very active and falls will hurt them, so handle them over a piece of furniture such as a settee.

EXERCISE

If your gerbils have plenty of playthings, then they should get plenty of exercise in the gerbilarium. It is safest not to let them free in a room or they might escape, but you can handle them regularly to tame them.

MALE OR FEMALE?

You can tell a male from a female gerbil the opposite way from hamsters. The end of the female's body is rounded, and the male's body points down to the tail.

BABIES

A pair of gerbils produce babies very quickly. If your female gives birth, do not touch the babies. At four weeks they can eat the same food as their mother, and at six weeks old the sexes should be separated, the babies taken away from their mother and good homes found for them.

HEALTH

Gerbils are very hardy and rarely get ill. If, however, you are worried about yours for any reason, then consult your vet.

Test Your Knowledge

Rearrange the letters at the beginning of each line to answer the question.

1. nagaor _____ A woolly rabbit?
2. yaris _____ Where all pet hamsters originally come from?
3. sabinisany _____ A breed of guinea pig?
4. tarnom _____ A hutch for exercising your pet rabbit?
5. tannolruc _____ Hamsters belong to this group?
6. imaruqua _____ Can make a good cage for some small pets?
7. icefratone _____ A digestive process in rabbits?
8. briligeramu _____ Where gerbils could live?

Cats

Cats are warm, soft and beautiful to look at. They can be very affectionate, playful and entertaining, and are quite cheap to feed. They also catch mice, which is why you will always find cats kept on a farm.

Cats enjoy company and do demand care and attention, but they also like to be independent. They are quite able to amuse themselves for large parts of the day without you, particularly if they have their own cat flap, so long as you feed them properly and give them a regular supply of water as well as cuddles and stroking sessions! A cat is very good at washing itself so you will never have to give it a bath, although you will need to keep its coat free from fleas. You will never need to take your cat for a walk, but you will need to make sure it has the proper injections to keep it free from disease.

A cat always likes to maintain a certain amount of independence, but a well-cared-for cat should keep you company for about twelve years.

WHICH CAT?

There are very many different varieties and colours of cats from which to choose. First you will have to decide whether you would like a long-haired or a short-haired cat. Long-haired demand more looking after than short-haired as they need grooming every day to keep their coats in good condition, although short-haired cats do need grooming as well.

The next thing to think about is whether you want to keep a pedigree or an ordinary mongrel (moggy) cat. Moggies have parents from different breeds, whereas pedigree cats have parents and ancestors from the same breed. Although pedigree cats are very beautiful, they are often highly strung. They are much more expensive to buy as well as to keep.

Here are some of the pedigree breeds you could choose from:

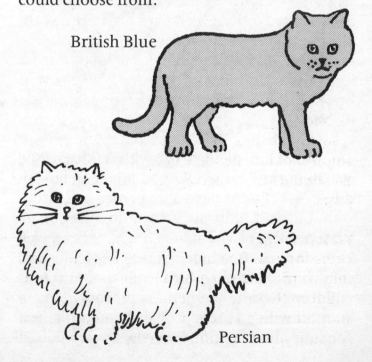

British Blue

Persian

Siamese

Burmese

Do you want to start off with a kitten and watch it grow, or would you prefer to buy an adult cat? Kittens need a lot of care and attention, but will probably grow into affectionate pets. A fully grown cat may not have been well cared for in its first home. It may be vicious and may bite or scratch strangers or boisterous children. On the whole, it is probably best to start off with a kitten, provided you can give it the time and attention it needs.

CHOOSING A KITTEN

You can buy kittens from pet shops, but many people whose cats have had kittens are happy to give them away to a good home. Look for adverts in newsagents' windows or on the notice-board in your local vet's. If possible, try to see the kitten with its mother so that you will know that the mother cat is healthy and well cared for.

A healthy kitten should:

1. Have bright eyes.
2. Have clean ears.
3. Have a full set of teeth.
4. Have a clean (not runny) nose.
5. Have a glossy coat.
6. Be clean and dry underneath its tail.

Kittens should be at least eight weeks old and fully weaned, i.e. on solid food before being taken from their mother. Ask the owner whether the kitten has been vaccinated against feline infectious enteritis. If your kitten catches this disease he will probably die, so it is important that the vaccination be given at about ten weeks old.

A KITTEN CARRIER

When you go to collect your kitten, you will need to take something to carry him home in. You could buy a cat-carrying basket or a cardboard carrier (you will need to use it again whenever you take your cat to the vet), or you could use a very strong cardboard box with a lid. Cut some air holes in the box and line it with newspaper. Make very sure that the kitten will not be able to escape. Kittens can squeeze through some very small holes!

AT HOME

When you get home, open the box or basket and let your kitten find his own way out. He may be a little frightened, so keep him in one room to start with. Make sure there are no escape routes (remember the chimney!). Let him run around and explore his new surroundings, but don't handle him too much at first.

You will need to buy or prepare some things for your new kitten.

KITTEN EQUIPMENT

Bed: You could spend a lot of money on a cat bed, but a cardboard box will be good enough. Cut a hole in one side to make it easy to get in and out. Line the box with newspaper and an old blanket or woolly jumper. If it is very cold, add a hot-water bottle (hand warm) wrapped in a blanket, so your kitten has something to snuggle up to.

Toilet: You can buy a cat-litter tray or use a baking tray (the sides should be about 8 cm high). Fill it with cat litter, which you can buy from most supermarkets, mixed with a bit of earth. Put the tray in a private corner on newspaper, in case of spillage.

Food Bowls: Two food bowls would be best so that one is always clean, and a water bowl. Make sure that they are not too deep or your kitten might not be able to reach the food.

Grooming: You will need to buy a soft brush, a metal comb, and some flea powder.

Scratching Post: Cats and kittens instinctively like to keep their claws sharp, as they are their hunting tools. Once your cat is old enough to go out on his own, he will probably sharpen his claws on a tree. To stop him sharpening his claws on the furniture indoors, you should provide him with a scratching post.

You could buy one, or you could make one by wrapping a length of wood in coarse parcel string. You will have to show your kitten how to use it.

Toys: Your kitten will find lots of things to play with. Try giving him a ping-pong ball, a scrunched-up ball of silver paper, a cotton reel, a ball of string or a big paper bag.

FOOD

Kittens cannot digest as much food as adult cats, so they need to be fed little and often. You should start with four meals a day and gradually cut down to three and then two as your kitten grows into a cat. Never feed a very young kitten tinned cat food, as it is too rich for him to digest. Two of the meals should be milk feeds, milk mixed with porridge or unsweetened breakfast cereal, and two minced meat: fish, chicken or rabbit. Always give fresh water to drink, and offer only as much food as your kitten can eat in five minutes.

HYGIENE

1. Always throw away any uneaten food and wash the eating dishes straight away in hot soapy water.
2. Change the litter in the litter tray regularly, or it will get smelly and your kitten will not want to use it.
3. If you have used a cardboard box as a bed, replace it from time to time (ask an adult to dispose of it for you). Replace the newspaper bedding regularly.
4. Keep cats off the kitchen table and work surfaces. Although they are very clean animals, they may carry germs.

IS YOUR HOME SAFE?

You may have heard of the saying 'curiosity

killed the cat'. Make sure it doesn't kill yours. Cats like to curl up in warm cosy places. Train your kitten not to sit on top of the grill or the oven. Always guard fireplaces or electric fires. Kittens also like to chew things, so train your kitten not to go on work-tops where he might play with or chew electric flexes.

● You need never smack a kitten or a cat. Simply say 'No' very firmly and take him away from the place that you do not want him to be.

GROOMING

Shorthairs: Cats and kittens usually enjoy being groomed and grooming certainly improves the appearance of the coat. Brush your short-haired regularly with a soft brush. Groom the tummy by laying your kitten on his back on your lap and gently brushing his tummy. Look out for fleas.

Longhairs: Longhairs need more grooming. Use a comb first to get out any tangles, and then give the coat a good brush, again looking out for fleas.

● If your cat does have fleas, then ask an adult to help you apply some flea powder. Follow the instructions on the packet and wash your hands carefully afterwards.

Instead of using flea powder, you could give your cat a flea collar to wear. Make sure it has an elastic insert, so that if your cat catches the collar on a branch he won't strangle himself.

TOILET TRAINING

Some mother cats teach their kittens to use the litter tray. If your kitten doesn't know how, then you will have to teach him. Put your kitten gently on the litter and show him how to make the litter move by using his front legs. If you think your kitten might want to use the tray, take him there and encourage him by talking to him.

Once your kitten has had all his innoculations and provided the weather is not too cold, you can train him to go outside to go to the toilet. Take your kitten to a soft spot of earth

and encourage him in the same way as you did with the cat tray. If he has an accident indoors, don't punish him. Instead, remind your kitten of what you would like him to do by taking him outside again.

CAT FLAP

Of course, if you want your cat or kitten to go outside on his own, then you must give him a cat flap. Teach him to use the cat flap by pushing him gently through it in both directions. Never force a cat to go out if he doesn't want to, especially at night. Always keep a cat or kitten indoors in his new home (even if he is an old pet and you have just moved house) for a month before allowing him to go outside, so that he doesn't get confused or lost.

PLAYING

Play with your kitten whenever he is feeling playful. As he gets older he will spend less time playing, but there is a toy you can make that cats and kittens will both love to play with.

Cats love the smell of catnip or catmint, which you can grow in a pot or in your garden. They love rubbing themselves in it and it is always guaranteed to give any cat a mad half hour!

To Make a Catnip Mouse

1. Draw around a large mug on a piece of material to make a circle.
2. Cut it out.
3. Cut the circle in half.

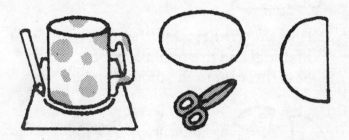

4. With the right side of the material on the inside, fold one of the pieces of material in half and sew along the straight edge.

5. Turn the right way out and stuff with dried catmint.

6. Sew the open edge together.

7. Cut the corners off the other piece of material and use to make ears.
8. Sew these on to the mouse's head.

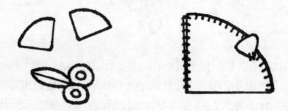

9. Cut a strip from the rest of the material and use to make a tail.

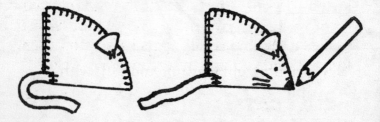

10. With a felt-tip pen, draw on a nose and whiskers.

• Give the mouse to your pet and see what happens!

HEALTH

If you look after your kitten well, he will probably be very healthy. Make sure he is vaccinated against feline infectious enteritis and cat flu, and keep an eye on his general health.

If you notice any soreness of the eyes or ears, coughing or sneezing, diarrhoea or vomiting, or worms passed when your pet goes to the toilet, then take him to the vet. Do not give worming tablets to a kitten without asking your vet first.

If your cat is a female (queen) and you do not want her to have kittens, you should have her spayed. Your vet will perform the operation for you and it can be done at any time from six months of age.

Male (tom) cats should also be neutered. As well as preventing them from fathering lots of kittens, it will stop them from marking their territory by spraying urine everywhere, which makes a terrible smell. It will also stop them fighting and straying in search of a mate.

ADULT CATS

Adult cats need the same sort of health care as kittens. They are more independent than kittens and should be fully toilet trained.

An adult cat needs two small meals or one large one a day. It is best to vary the food you give them, and a good tinned cat food is often as good as home cooking. If you feed your cat dried food, then make sure he always has plenty of water available.

MORE KITTENS

If you have not had your queen spayed and she is expecting babies, make sure she eats well and that there is a cardboard box lined with newspaper available for her to use as a nest. She may well not use it and choose somewhere else such as the airing cupboard instead! Kittens are born sixty-five days after mating and unless there are complications, the mother will not need any help at all. She should, however, be given about three times as much to eat as usual while she is feeding her kittens. The nest should be disturbed as little as possible until the kittens are old enough to leave it, as the mother will keep it clean. By four weeks old, the kittens will be leaving the nest, and by eight weeks old they should be weaned. You will then be able to look for homes for the ones you do not want to keep.

A Catty Crossword

Across
1. Neutering of female.
2. Daily food.
3. A deadly disease.
4. Female cat.

Down
1. Toilet.
2. High-class ancestry.
3. Exotic cat.
4. Favourite plant.

Dogs

Have you ever heard the saying 'a dog is a man's best friend'? Dogs are great company and loyal friends. They will guard you or your home, but in return they need company and friendship, as well as food, care and exercise every day.

You will be legally responsible for your dog's behaviour wherever you go, so it is up to you to train it to behave properly and to keep it under control. This will take time and patience.

Owning a dog is not cheap as they eat more than most pets, and will certainly keep you fit! It is very rewarding though, and once you do own a dog you can never be lonely or lazy!

CHOOSING A DOG

Deciding which dog to have as your pet can be very difficult, because there are so many different types from which to choose. The first thing that you need to decide is whether you want to have an adult dog or a puppy. A puppy will be more messy, more mischievous and need more care to start off with than a fully grown dog, but, because it has been trained by you, it will know the rules of your home and fit in with your family better than a dog who has been trained by someone else.

WHICH PUPPY?

How much space have you got at home? Do you live in the town or the country? How much exercise do you like? A small puppy may grow into a very large dog, so before buying your puppy think how big a dog you want to end up with. The larger the dog, the more it will eat and the more exercise it will need.

Do you want a pedigree dog or a mongrel? Pedigree dogs have both parents and ancestors of the same breed and can be entered for shows. Mongrels have parents from different breeds. It can be difficult to tell what a mongrel puppy is eventually going to look like, unless you know who both its parents are, but they usually make friendly family dogs.

A pedigree will be more expensive to buy and there are hundreds of different sorts from which to choose. Here are just a few.

Small Dogs

Dachshund   Poodle

Chihuahua

Beagle

Corgi

Scottish Terrier

Medium Dogs

Shetland Sheepdog

Schnauzer

Cocker Spaniel

Airedale

Large Dogs

Alsatian
Retriever

Labrador

Old English Sheepdog

Before finally deciding, ask the breeder how much exercise the dog will need, how much it will eat, and how much you will have to groom it. Make sure that you will be able to care for it.

MALE OR FEMALE?

Do you want a male or a female dog? Bitches (female dogs) tend to be more affectionate and easier to train than male dogs, but they might present you with unwanted puppies. They will need spaying to prevent this.

HOW TO CHOOSE A HEALTHY PUPPY

Choose a puppy who is bright, alert and inquisitive. She should be sturdy and not at all nervous. Puppies should be at least eight weeks of age before being taken away from their mother.

You can buy a puppy from a pet shop, dealer, breeder, private home or dogs' home. It is best to buy from the person who bred the puppy so that you can see the mother, who should look healthy and well cared for.

PICKING A PUPPY UP

Puppies are very delicate and easily hurt. It is very important that you know how to pick your puppy up properly. Put one hand firmly under your puppy's bottom and the other under her chest. Keep the weight evenly balanced between both hands. Never pick a puppy up by the legs or neck.

TAKING YOUR PUPPY HOME

A puppy is as helpless and vulnerable as a human baby. When you begin owning her, it will be the first time she has left her mother and brothers and sisters, and she is likely to be very unhappy. You will need to be very gentle, patient and comforting. If your puppy is going to travel home with you by car, take a warm blanket to wrap her up in and a warm, wrapped hot-water bottle for her to snuggle up to. Don't be surprised if she is sick. If you are walking or travelling by public transport, you will need to take a pet carrier with you. Line it with newspaper or a towel (a blanket will take up too much room).

When you get home, there should be a special place ready for your puppy. This will be where she goes to sleep or when she wants to be quiet.

PUPPY EQUIPMENT

Bed: You do not need to buy a dog basket or a special bed for your puppy. She will only grow out of it or eat it! Until your puppy is fully grown, a sturdy cardboard box makes a very comfortable bed. Turn it on its side and put a towel or a blanket that is easy to wash in it for bedding. The sides of the box will keep your puppy cosy, but you should also place the bed away from draughts.

Food Bowls: You will need two bowls, one for water and one for food. Your puppy should always eat from her own bowls and never from yours. Heavy earthenware bowls are best as they are difficult to tip up.

Toys: These are very important. As a puppy will probably chew anything that you give her, you should make sure that all the toys are safe and that she cannot choke. Remember that if you give your puppy an old shoe or slipper to chew, she will then expect to be allowed to chew any shoe or slipper that she finds in the house. This might make her and you very unpopular!

Newspaper: Your puppy is a baby and will not be toilet trained. She is likely to make quite a bit of mess, so you will need to have a good supply of newspaper to cover the floor with.

Playpen: If you can't find or borrow one of these, it is not essential. If your puppy can wander freely around the house, there will be quite a few things that she could hurt herself on (electric flexes, for example). If she gets in the way in the kitchen, she may get scalded or burned. An old child's playpen is a good way of keeping her (and the mess!) in one place, while giving her plenty of freedom to move around.

Name: It is a good idea to have a name ready for your puppy as soon as possible, so that you can use it and she will get used to it. Shorter names are best.

Name Tag: When your puppy is eventually allowed to go out on the street, the law requires that she wears her name and address. This could be on an engraved metal disc or on a piece of paper inside a holder. Both can be worn on a collar.

Collar and Lead: Before you take your puppy out for walks, you will need to get her used to a collar and lead. Ask in a pet shop which type is best for your puppy. A fully grown dog will need a different and stronger collar and lead.

SETTLING YOUR PUPPY IN

When you first get your puppy home, she may be anxious and unhappy. You will need to take the place of her mother until she settles in. Nurse your puppy and talk gently to her. She may like to have a sleep in her bed and again a warm hot-water bottle can help. When she wakes up, offer her a bowl of warm milk and cereal. She will need a lot of quiet attention at first and may not want to play.

Even a confident puppy who wants to play still needs to be treated very gently. Puppies, like babies, need a lot of sleep. At night-time your puppy may cry and be very unhappy, even if you have done everything you can think of to help. Try putting your puppy's bed next to yours, so she knows she isn't alone. Once she has settled down in your home, she will sleep where you want her to. Never scold your puppy in the first week and never, ever hit her. It is during the first few weeks at home that you will build up trust and confidence with your dog that will last for ever.

FOOD

A small puppy needs four meals a day. Two should be milk and breakfast cereal, and two should be meat. For the meat meals, mix minced meat or fish with biscuit or bread. Instead you can buy specially prepared puppy food. Only give your puppy as much as she can eat in five minutes. Always clear away any uneaten food and wash the bowl in hot soapy water straight away. If food is allowed to go stale, your puppy might get diarrhoea.

As your puppy grows, reduce the number of meals and make each meal bigger. By eight months she should have a meat meal morning and evening. Always make sure fresh water is available. By eighteen months feed only one main meal a day of meat or tinned dog food mixed with biscuit or cereal, and a snack in the morning of a little milk and a few biscuits.

HOUSE TRAINING

This takes time and patience. Never smack your puppy or rub her nose in any mess she has produced, as this will only confuse and upset her.

Start house training as soon as you get your puppy home. Always be patient and never shout. Introduce your puppy to the garden; take her outside and stay with her until she goes to the toilet. When she does, give her lots of praise and pat her very gently. Your puppy will soon learn that the garden is the place to use, but will still not be able to tell you when she needs to go to the toilet. You will need to be very observant.

Whenever your puppy squats down or is looking for somewhere to squat, pick her up, take her outside and stay with her. When she has finished, praise her again. Never tell your puppy off unless you actually catch her in the act, in which case a sharp 'No!' should be enough to stop her until you take her outside. At night-time you will need to put plenty of newspaper down, unless you want to stay up all night to let your puppy out! Take her out first thing in the morning and after a meal. Have patience – house training can be a slow process and may even take months.

EXERCISE

Young puppies don't need long walks as they can get overtired. Until she is four months old, it is enough to let your puppy run around in the garden as much as she wants to. More exercise might be necessary with a very large breed of dog, so ask the breeder for advice. When your puppy is four months old, take her to a large grassy area such as a park and let her run off steam away from the danger of traffic.

You should let your puppy sleep as much as she wants to during the day. Never force her to play or go for a walk.

HEALTH

It is very important to have your puppy vaccinated against killer diseases. Until you have done so and your vet has told you that it is safe, don't take your puppy to any place where she might come into contact with other dogs or where dogs might have been.

You should have your puppy checked by your vet as soon as you can, just to make sure that she is in good health. Your vet will advise you as to which injections are necessary and at what age, in order to protect your puppy. The vet will also advise you about worming.

If your puppy is a bitch and you do not want her to have puppies later in life, your vet will also advise you about having her neutered. A bitch first comes into season at about six months old and then twice every year. She will be in season for about three weeks each time, so you will have to keep a careful eye on her to make sure that she doesn't mate with a dog if you do not want her to. Male dogs can also be neutered.

You should watch your puppy for any sign of illness. Look out for runny eyes; a runny nose or a temperature; vomiting or diarrhoea; worms or parasites. If you are at all worried about your dog's health, ask your vet's advice.

TRAINING AND OBEDIENCE

If you would like some help in training your puppy or dog, you could enrol for a dog obedience class. This might be useful if you are hoping to 'show' your dog later. There are some things that you must teach your puppy at an early stage, if you want to be confident that you can control her.

Collar and Lead Training: When your puppy is about three months old, you should teach her to wear a collar and to walk on a lead. Let her get used to wearing a collar before you try using a lead. Make sure that the collar isn't too tight. A good test is to make sure you can easily slip a finger underneath the collar while it is being worn. Once your puppy is happy with this, fit the lead. Keep the lead slack, walk away from your puppy and say 'Come'. Give a very gentle pull on the lead. When your puppy walks towards you, praise her.

Next try walking a few steps with the lead. Hold it in your left hand and again say 'Come', as you begin to walk. Encourage your puppy to keep up with you, not pulling or stopping at every fence! Never jerk your puppy back, but pull her firmly and say 'Heel'. Praise her enthusiastically whenever she succeeds.

'Come': It is very important that your dog learns to come to you when you call her,

otherwise you will never be able to let her off the lead. Use her name and say 'Come', patting your knees at the same time. Start with a short distance only and praise your dog or reward her when she does come to you.

'Sit': Teach your dog to sit by saying 'Sit', and press on her bottom at the same time. If you praise her when she gets it right, your dog will soon sit on command. This is a useful command when you are waiting to cross the road. When you are ready to cross say 'Over', and pull gently on the lead.

'No!': If it is ever really necessary to reprimand your dog, say 'No!' firmly and shake the skin on the back of her neck. Never hit your dog.

ADULT DOGS

As your puppy grows into a dog she will need less constant attention, but you will still need to look after her well.

GROOMING

All adult dogs need regular grooming to keep their coat clean and healthy. What kind of grooming tools you need depends on what kind of coat your dog has. Ask your breeder or vet for advice.

You should only give your dog a bath if it is really necessary. Use a mild shampoo and don't get it in your dog's eyes or mouth.

FOOD

In addition to a main meat meal and a light snack every day, you might like to give your dog a treat by giving her a bone. She will really enjoy gnawing at it and it will be good exercise for her teeth. Do not give chicken or small chop bones as these might splinter or stick in her throat. You can expect an angry reaction if you try to take your dog's bone away!

BED

Once your dog is fully grown, you should provide her with a proper bed. There are many different types from which to choose, but the bed should be big enough for your dog to curl up in comfortably (this is how she keeps herself warm). Plastic beds are easiest to keep clean as they can be washed. As with a puppy, use a blanket or towel as bedding.

COLLAR

Once your dog is fully grown, you will need to buy her a new collar and a strong lead. A long leather lead with a strong clip is reliable for most dogs, but you might need a short leather strap to control a very large dog. Instead of a collar, a large dog could wear a chain. Make sure you put it on properly or you could choke your dog by pulling too tightly on the lead. (See diagram.)

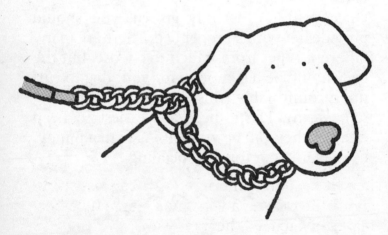

BABIES

If you decide to mate your bitch or she does get pregnant, you will need to take good care of her and make sure that she eats well. She will begin to look fatter and her teats will swell. Puppies will be born about seven weeks after mating.

A few days before the puppies are due, ask your vet to give your dog a check-up. Prepare a box as a bed and line it with plenty of newspaper. If all goes well, the mother will need no help. If she is in difficulty call the vet. The mother will wash the puppies off herself by licking them roughly (this also helps them to breathe properly). She will care for the babies herself so don't interfere. You can assist by giving the mother a very good diet to help her make milk to feed the pups with.

After about ten days the puppies' eyes will open. You should make sure they get used to hearing human voices by speaking quietly to them. They should be taught to lap milk and eat very finely minced meat by eight weeks old, and they will be big enough to get out of their bed. Make sure there is plenty of newspaper on the floor as the puppies won't be house trained. You will need to find good homes for the puppies you don't want to keep.

WORKING DOGS

Some dogs work for a living, as well as being pets. Do you know which breeds of dogs do these jobs? (Answers at bottom of page.)

1. Police dog.
2. Guide dog for the blind.
3. Mountain rescue.
4. Herding sheep.
5. Hearing dogs for the deaf.

Did You Know?
When a bitch has puppies it is called 'whelping', and the mother dog is called a 'dam'.
Dogs sweat through their paw pads. This leaves a scent on the ground that other dogs can follow.

Answers
1. Alsatian 2. Labrador or Retriever 3. St Bernard 4. Collie 5. Jack Russell terrier.

Useful Addresses

Royal Society for the Prevention of
Cruelty to Animals
Junior Membership:
Causeway, Horsham, Sussex RH12 1HG

Royal Society for the Protection of Birds
Young Ornithologists' Club:
The Lodge, Sandy, Beds.

People's Dispensary for Sick Animals
Busy Bees Club:
Unit 6B, Ketley Business Park,
Telford, Shropshire TF1 4JD

British Veterinary Association,
7 Mansfield St, London W1M 0AT

Kennel Club,
1 Clarges St, London W1Y 8AB

National Dog Owners' Association,
92 High St, Lee-on-Solent,
Hants PO13 9BU

Cat Protection League,
29 Church St, Slough, Berks.

Index